DECONSTRUCTING POWERFUL SPEECHES

IDA B. WELLS

LYNCHING, OUR NATIONAL CRIME

REBECCA SJONGER

CRABTREE
PUBLISHING COMPANY
WWW.CRABTREEBOOKS.COM

CRABTREE
PUBLISHING COMPANY
WWW.CRABTREEBOOKS.COM

Author:
Rebecca Sjonger
Series research and development:
Janine Deschenes and Ellen Rodger
Editorial director:
Kathy Middleton
Editor:
Ellen Rodger
Proofreader:
Roseann Biederman
Graphic design:
Katherine Berti
Image research:
Rebecca Sjonger and Katherine Berti
Print coordinator:
Katherine Berti

Images:
Abraham Lincoln Presidential Library and Museum: p. 4–5 (top), 5 (inset)
Alamy
dbimages: p. 42–43
Jason O. Watson: p. 7
The Protected Art Archive: p. 8–9 (top), 11 (top right)
Associated Press, Mary Hattler: p. 38 (bottom)
Black Past, Timothy Willis: p. 16
Chicago Tribune: p. 24 (top)
Georgia State University: p. 39 (top)
Getty Images, Stan Wayman: p. 29 (bottom)
Internet Archive, Proceedings of the National Negro Conference 1909: p. 12 (bottom right)
Library of Congress: p. 21 (top), 24 (bottom), 30 (right), 36 (bottom)
Rare Book and Special Collections Division, Printed Ephemera Collection: p. 34
Lincoln Library, Sangamon Valley Collection: p. 4–5 (bottom)
National Archives: p. 17, 30 (left)
General Records of the Department of Justice: p. 10 (top)
The National Guard, Rick Reeves: p. 22–23
New York Public Library: p. 20 (center)
Shutterstock, Tverdokhlib: p. 9 (bottom)
University of Chicago Library, Special Collections Research Center: p. 3, 6 (bottom left), 20 (bottom left, right), 27 (bottom), 32, 41 (bottom)
The White House, President Barack Obama: p. 41 (top)
Wikimedia Commons
The American Review of Reviews, Volume 38, Independence Party of the United States: p. 35
Beyond My Ken: p. 6 (top right), 11 (bottom left)
Bibliothèque nationale de France: p. 31
Flickr, 08KKKfamilyPortrait: p. 21 (bottom)
King of Hearts: p. 39 (bottom)
Lawson Andrew Scruggs: p. 1
Library of Congress: p. 13
National Archives and Records Administration, Goerge Kendall Warren: p. 37
New York Public Library Digital Collection: p. 28
New York Times: p. 11 (bottom right)/
Omnia Williams: p. 38 (top)
Project Gutenberg ebook of Sparkling Gems of Race Knowledge Worth Reading: p. 11 (top left)
Segregation. AAPF. Accessed October 11, 2018. www.aapf.org:segregation: p. 36 (top)
Ser Amantio di Nicolao: p. 6 (bottom right)
Thomas R Machnitzki: p. 27 (top)
USIA, National Archives and Records Administration Records of the U.S. Information Agency Record Group 306: p. 29 (top)
www.lib.uchicago.edu, Screen Shot 2020-06-18 at 4.57.32 PM: p. 12 (bottom left)
All other images by Shutterstock

Library and Archives Canada Cataloguing in Publication

Title: Ida B. Wells : lynching, our national crime / Rebecca Sjonger.
Names: Sjonger, Rebecca, author.
Series: Sjonger, Rebecca. Deconstructing powerful speeches.
Description: Series statement: Deconstructing powerful speeches | Includes bibliographical references and index.
Identifiers: Canadiana (print) 20200289950 | Canadiana (ebook) 20200290010 | ISBN 9780778781646 (softcover) | ISBN 9780778781608 (hardcover) | ISBN 9781427125903 (HTML)
Subjects: LCSH: Wells-Barnett, Ida B., 1862-1931—Oratory—Juvenile literature. | LCSH: African Americans—Civil rights—History—Juvenile literature. | LCSH: Lynching—United States—History—Juvenile literature. | LCSH: United States—Race relations—History—Juvenile literature. | LCSH: Speeches, addresses, etc., American—History and criticism—Juvenile literature. | LCSH: Oratory—United States—Juvenile literature.
Classification: LCC E185.61 .S56 2021 | DDC j323.1196073—dc23

Library of Congress Cataloging-in-Publication Data

Names: Sjonger, Rebecca, author.
Title: Ida B. Wells : lynching, our national crime / Rebecca Sjonger.
Description: New York, NY : Crabtree Publishing Company, [2021] | Series: Deconstructing powerful speeches | Includes bibliographical references and index.
Identifiers: LCCN 2020031629 (print) | LCCN 2020031630 (ebook) | ISBN 9780778781608 (hardcover) | ISBN 9780778781646 (paperback) | ISBN 9781427125903 (ebook)
Subjects: LCSH: Wells-Barnett, Ida B., 1862-1931. Lynching, our national crime--Juvenile literature. | Lynching--United States--History--Juvenile literature. | Lynching--Southern States--History--Juvenile literature. | Speeches, addresses, etc., American--Juvenile literature.
Classification: LCC HV6457.W393 S56 2021 (print) | LCC HV6457.W393 (ebook) | DDC 364.1/34--dc23
LC record available at https://lccn.loc.gov/2020031629
LC ebook record available at https://lccn.loc.gov/2020031630

Crabtree Publishing Company
www.crabtreebooks.com 1-800-387-7650

Printed in the U.S.A./092020/CG20200810

Published in Canada
Crabtree Publishing
616 Welland Ave.
St. Catharines, Ontario
L2M 5V6

Published in the United States
Crabtree Publishing
347 Fifth Ave
Suite 1402-145
New York, NY 10016

Published in the United Kingdom
Crabtree Publishing
Maritime House
Basin Road North, Hove
BN41 1WR

Published in Australia
Crabtree Publishing
3 Charles Street
Coburg North
VIC 3058

CONTENTS

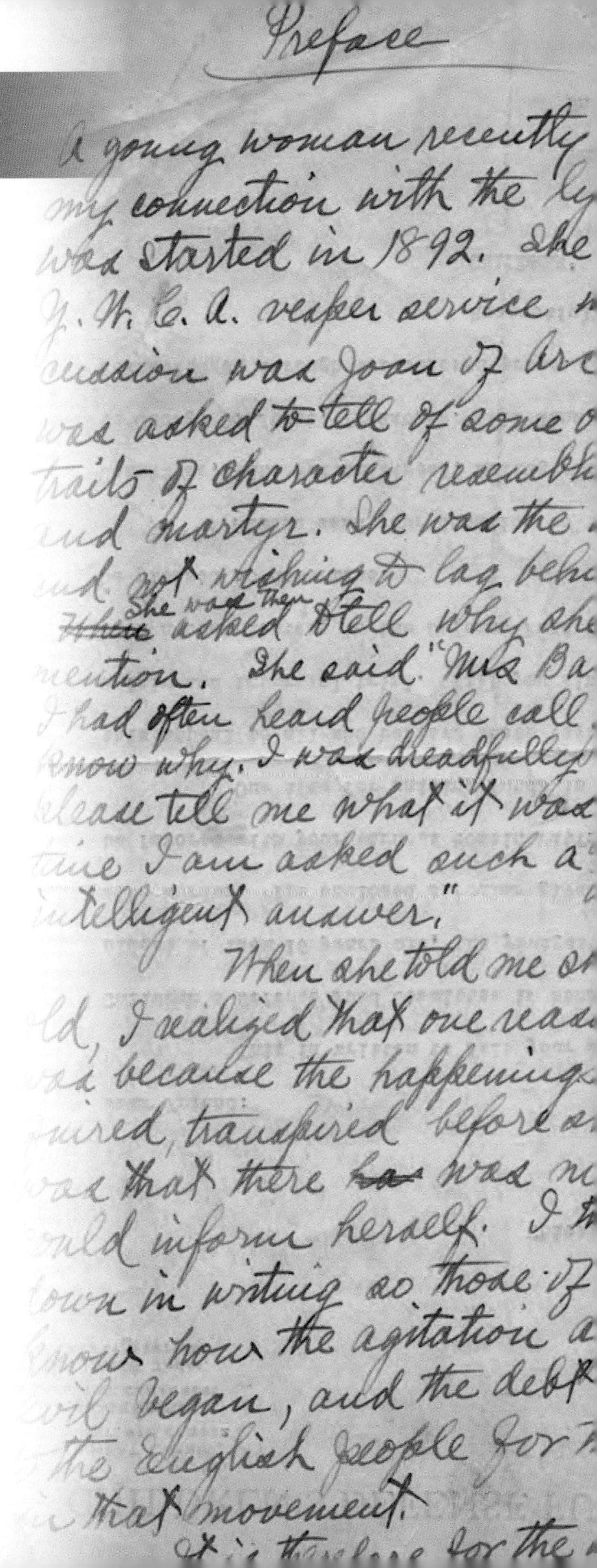
Preface

A young woman recently
my connection with the ly
was started in 1892. She
Y.W.C.A. vesper service
casion was Joan of Arc
was asked to tell of some
traits of character resembl
and martyr. She was the
and not wishing to lag beh
She was then asked to tell why she
mention. She said "Mrs Ba
I had often heard people call
know why. I was dreadfully
please tell me what it was
time I am asked such a
intelligent answer."
When she told me s
old, I realized that one reas
was because the happening
transpired before
was that there was n
could inform herself. I th
down in writing so those of
know how the agitation a
evil began, and the debt
the English people for
that movement.

INTRODUCTION

It was Friday afternoon in the summer of 1908. Sheriff Charles Werner watched as a **mob** gathered around the jail in Springfield, Illinois. Two African American men were held there. Joe James was accused of murder and George Richardson of **rape**. The victims of both crimes were white. Now a large crowd wanted to lynch the prisoners.

Lynching punished people with no concern for the law. Groups banded together to torture, hang, burn, or shoot them. Sometimes, they did all of these things. The lynchers were usually white. Their targets, overwhelmingly Black.

SPRINGFIELD RACE RIOT

The sheriff secretly moved James and Richardson out of the city to prevent their lynchings. The mob was angry when they found out that evening. They lashed out at the African Americans who lived in Springfield. Hundreds were hurt. Homes and businesses were burned down. The crowd of mostly working-class white men took out their rage on innocent people such as William Donnegan. The successful business owner was in his eighties. The lynchers dragged him from his home. They beat him with bricks and slit his throat with a razor. His lifeless body was left hanging from a tree.

Thwarted in their attempts to grab the prisoners, white mobs set fire to Black homes and businesses in Springfield. The days of white on Black violence that followed became known as the Springfield Race Riot.

*Two Black men were lynched in the mob violence. Several lynchers were killed by the state's **militia**. The troops spent two days trying to end the rioting.*

The Springfield mob likely targeted businessman William Donnegan (pictured here as a young man) because of his wealth and success.

THE NATIONAL NEGRO CONFERENCE

The violence in Springfield sparked the fight for **civil rights**. African Americans needed justice. **Activists** began to meet and make plans. The National Negro Conference brought together people who wanted to end lynching and other forms of **racial discrimination**. The Henry Street Settlement House in New York City hosted the conference. It took place on May 31 and June 1, 1909. It included speeches, presentations of scientific papers, and debates on how to bring about change.

Henry Street Settlement in New York City was a community center and meeting place.

When Wells married in 1895, her full name became Ida Bell Wells-Barnett. She also used the name Iola as a writer.

The house where Ida B. Wells was born, in Holly Springs, Mississippi, is now the Ida B. Wells-Barnett Museum.

REPORTING ON RACISM

Ida B. Wells was at the conference. She was born into slavery in Mississippi in 1862, and freed with her family after the **Emancipation Proclamation** was passed that same year. Ida was the eldest of eight children and her parents worked hard to establish themselves after freedom. By the time she was 16, her parents and one sibling had died in a **yellow fever** epidemic. Ida, who had attended college, took a teaching job to support the family. Ida knew well the **indignities** of racial discrimination. She spoke out against it in her daily life, and began writing about it in newspapers in her early twenties. One event spurred her to focus on a the particular injustice of lynching. Her friend, Thomas Moss, was murdered by a mob 1892. He and his business partners at Peoples Grocery were seen as competition for customers by a white-owned store. After a group of angry white men came to confront them at their store, the business partners were arrested. Masked men later took them from their cells and shot them. Wells covered lynching in the *Memphis Free Speech and Headlight,* a newspaper she partly owned. A **biographer** called her one of the first **investigative reporters**. She fled north for safety after the paper's office was destroyed.

THE CRIME OF LYNCHING

At forty-six, Ida B. Wells was a leader in anti-lynching campaigns. She spoke about it at the National Negro Conference. Her **address** was titled "Lynching, Our National Crime." She argued that lynching was murder. This crime was committed against defenseless people who had either committed no crime at all or were awaiting trial on charges. Wells proved false the often-used justification for lynching Black men—that they had attacked white women. She researched the real motivation for lynching. The purpose of her speech was to expose lynching as racism backed up by lies. She wanted to persuade the country to protect all citizens against it. The audience at the conference shared many of Wells's views. Her **argument** was also meant to spread to all Americans. They were deeply divided on race-related issues.

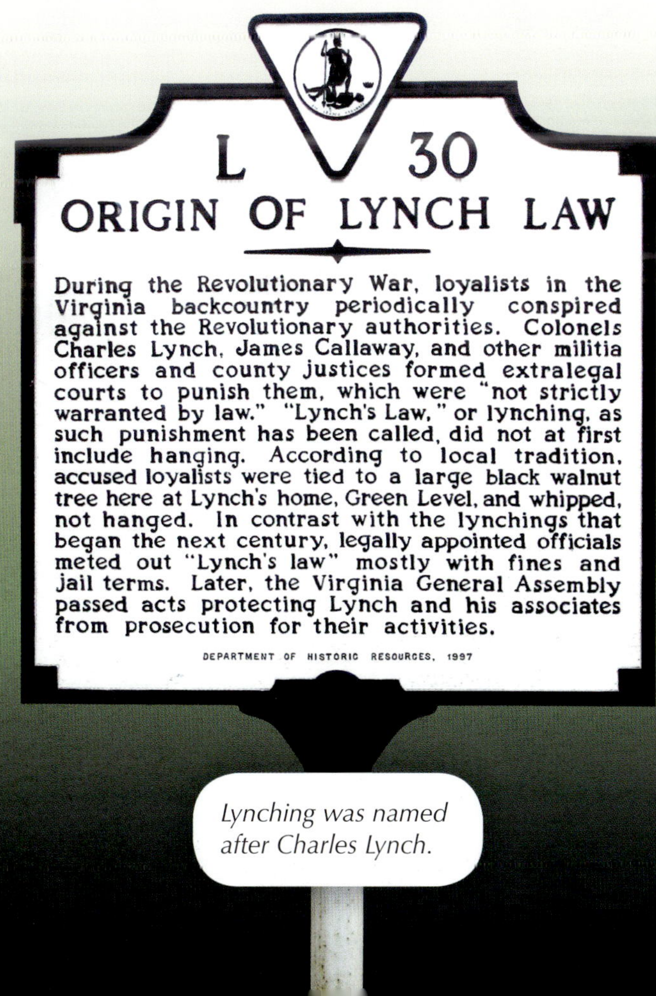

Lynching was named after Charles Lynch.

READ IT

"Lynching, Our National Crime" is over 1,600 words long. Sources like this book and most websites focus on key sections of it. Iowa State University provides the full text of the speech: **https://bit.ly/3dOieir**

The National Association for the Advancement of Colored People (NAACP) was founded in 1909. It led a 30-year campaign against lynching. Wells did much to establish the organization, but her name is not included in the list of founders. It is now the oldest and largest civil rights organization in the United States that aims to ensure equal rights and justice.

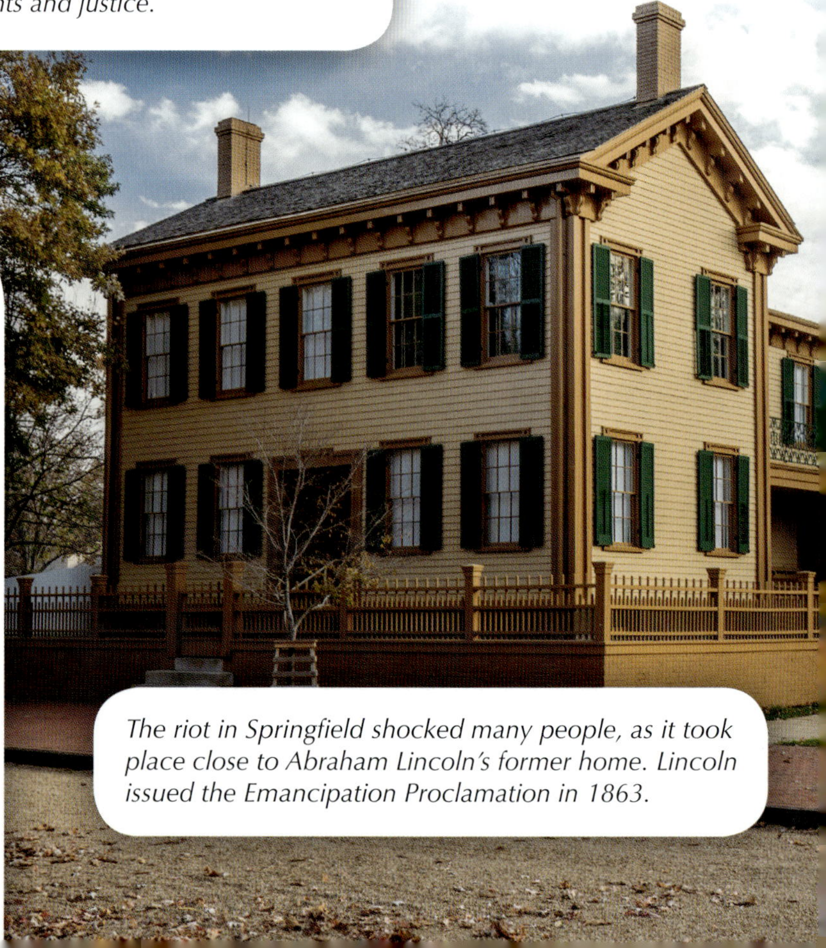

The riot in Springfield shocked many people, as it took place close to Abraham Lincoln's former home. Lincoln issued the Emancipation Proclamation in 1863.

TIMELINE

1862	July 16, Ida B. Wells born
1865	February 1, American government ends slavery
1865	April 9, American Civil War ended
1896	Wells co-founded National Association of Colored Women
1908	August 14-16, Riot in Springfield, Illinois
1909	National Association for the Advancement of Colored People (NAACP) formed
1931	March 25, Wells died

CHALLENGES AND OPPORTUNITIES

Today, many would argue lynching has transformed into different forms of racial terror. **Prejudices** against African Americans as well as Latinos, Muslims, Jews and other people not seen as white continue to fuel **inequality** and violence. Ida B. Wells's call to solve these issues as a country are just as relevant today. Her courage and determination continue to inspire.

DIGGING DEEPER

Some terms used in the past are offensive now. Do you think they should be changed for today's audiences? Why or why not?

PERSUASIVE PRIMARY SOURCES

Ida B. Wells's speech is an example of a primary source. These sources are original, firsthand accounts. The **U.S. Library of Congress** calls them "raw materials." They include text, images, and audio files, such as letters written by Wells and photos of her. Primary sources bring us as close as we can get to a historical event or time period. For example, the data in public polls reveals people's opinions in the past. Wells's speech about lynching exposes race-based injustice in the United States in the late 1800s and early 1900s.

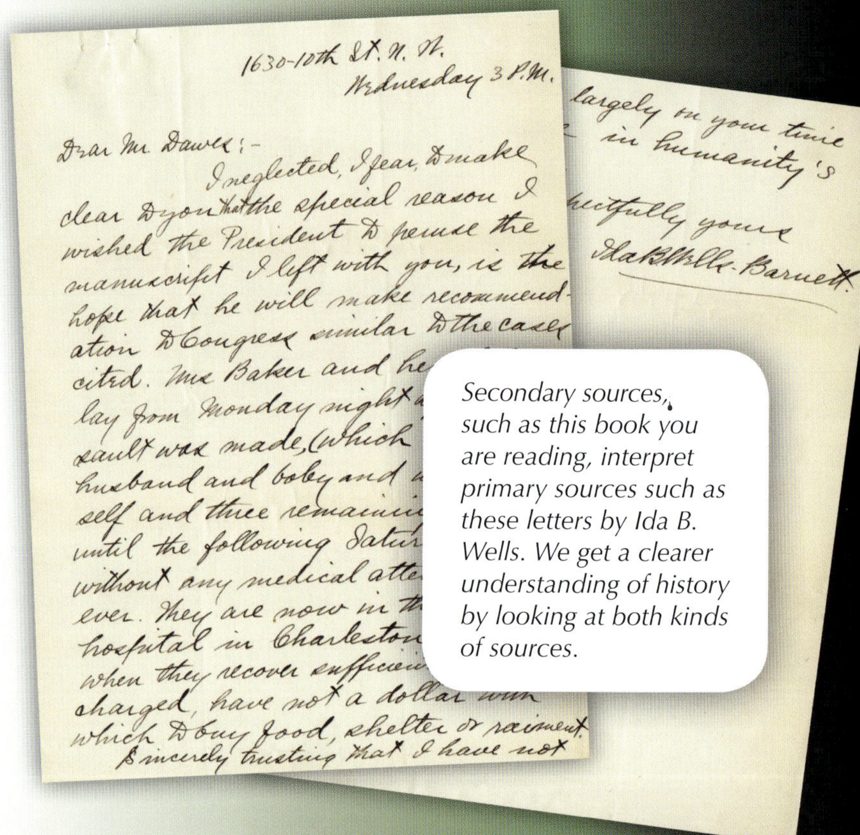

1630-10th St. N. W.
Wednesday 3 P.M.

Dear Mr. Dawes:-
I neglected, I fear, to make clear to you that the special reason I wished the President to peruse the manuscript I left with you, is the hope that he will make recommendation to Congress similar to the cases cited. Mrs Baker and he
lay from Monday night
sault was made, (which
husband and baby and
self and three remaini
until the following Satur
without any medical atte
ever. They are now in th
hospital in Charleston
when they recover sufficie
charged, have not a dollar with which to buy food, shelter or raiment.
Sincerely trusting that I have not

largely on your time
in humanity's
pectfully yours
Ida B. Wells-Barnett.

Secondary sources, such as this book you are reading, interpret primary sources such as these letters by Ida B. Wells. We get a clearer understanding of history by looking at both kinds of sources.

A WIDER LOOK

Secondary sources shed light on and explain primary sources. These materials may review an event, **analyze** someone's words, or share an opinion. They could use multiple sources to give more context. Allowing time to pass often affects how these materials approach the subject. Books about civil rights and profiles that describe Ida B. Wells's life are examples of secondary resources.

Have you ever made a video? If so, you created a primary source!

FIND THE FACTS

The first step in analyzing a primary source is checking a few basic details. Gather the following facts:

Maker, such as a writer

***Intended** audience*

Date it was created

Purpose

Place it was delivered

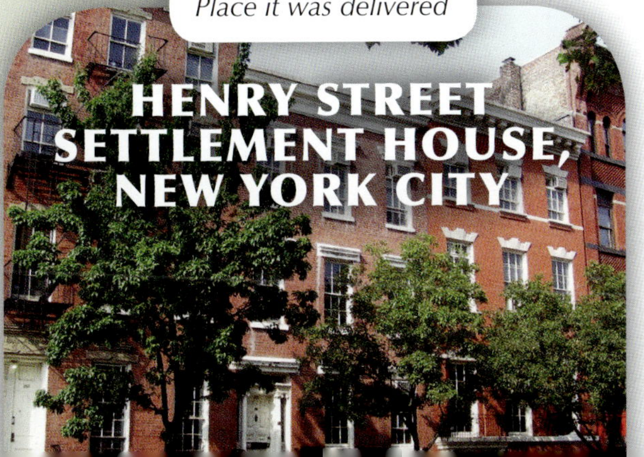

Maker's point of view

LYNCHING WAS MURDER

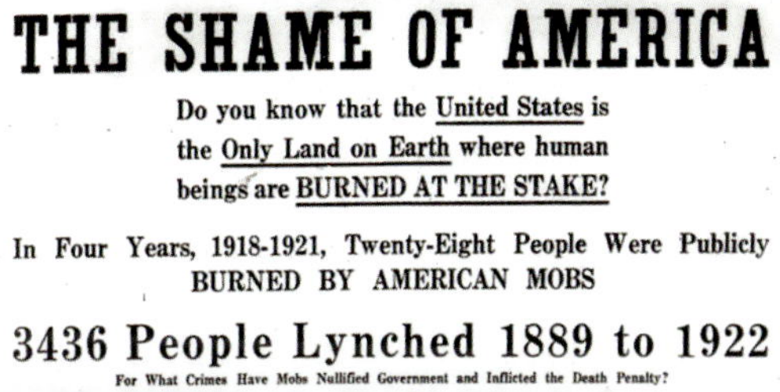

THE SHAME OF AMERICA

Do you know that the United States is the Only Land on Earth where human beings are BURNED AT THE STAKE?

In Four Years, 1918-1921, Twenty-Eight People Were Publicly BURNED BY AMERICAN MOBS

3436 People Lynched 1889 to 1922

For What Crimes Have Mobs Nullified Government and Inflicted the Death Penalty?

COLLECTING CLUES

Primary sources do not always reveal the facts needed to assess them. For example, while the purpose and Ida B. Wells's point of view are clear in her speech, details such as the date and place it was delivered are not listed. If this information is available, it may be found in cataloging information. Libraries and other organizations collect data about their sources. It is entered into a catalog, or database. These tools are especially helpful when studying historical materials.

WRITTEN FORM

Details about speeches may also be found in transcripts. These are printed versions. In the past, they were handwritten as the words were spoken or later from memory. A speaker's own notes could also become a transcript. Without audio or video recordings of historical speeches, transcripts are the only form available to study.

The University of Chicago Library Guide to the Ida B. Wells Papers, *makes the date and context of a primary source clear to readers.*

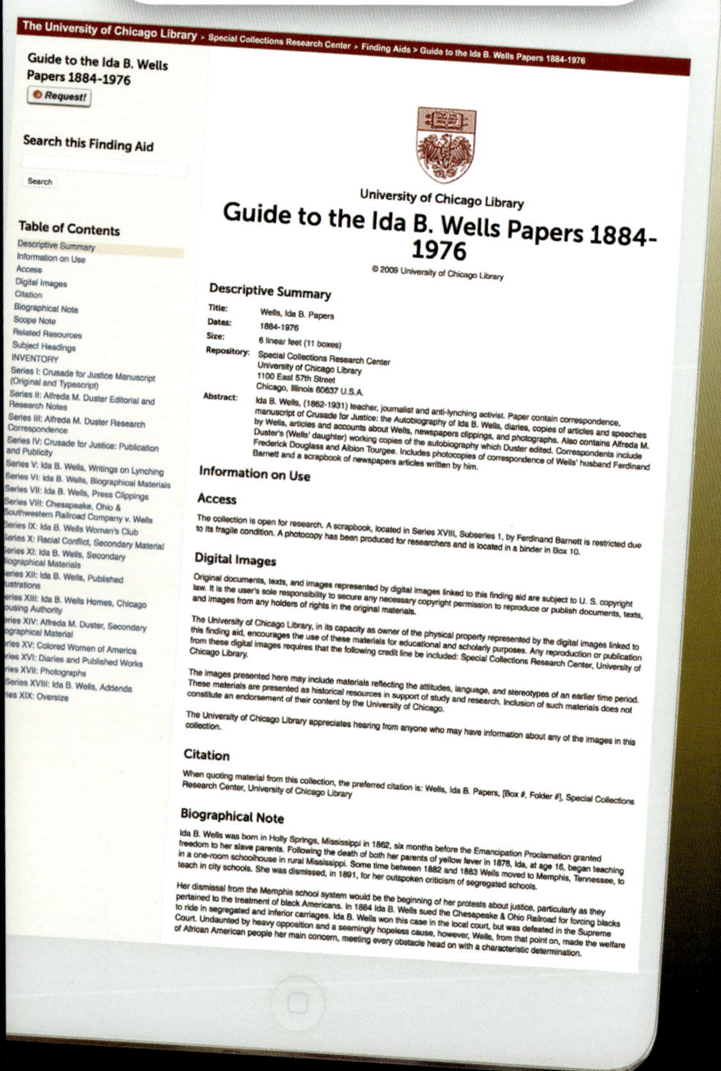

The University of Chicago Library > Special Collections Research Center > Finding Aids > Guide to the Ida B. Wells Papers 1884-1976

Guide to the Ida B. Wells Papers 1884-1976

Request!

Search this Finding Aid

Search

Table of Contents

Descriptive Summary
Information on Use
Access
Digital Images
Citation
Biographical Note
Scope Note
Related Resources
Subject Headings
INVENTORY
Series I: Crusade for Justice Manuscript (Original and Typescript)
Series II: Alfreda M. Duster Editorial and Research Notes
Series III: Alfreda M. Duster Research Correspondence
Series IV: Crusade for Justice: Publication and Publicity
Series V: Ida B. Wells, Writings on Lynching
Series VI: Ida B. Wells, Biographical Materials
Series VII: Ida B. Wells, Press Clippings
Series VIII: Chesapeake, Ohio & Southwestern Railroad Company v. Wells
Series IX: Ida B. Wells Woman's Club
Series X: Racial Conflict, Secondary Material
Series XI: Ida B. Wells, Secondary Biographical Materials
Series XII: Ida B. Wells, Published Illustrations
Series XIII: Ida B. Wells Homes, Chicago Housing Authority
Series XIV: Alfreda M. Duster, Secondary Biographical Material
Series XV: Colored Women of America
Series XVI: Diaries and Published Works
Series XVII: Photographs
Series XVIII: Ida B. Wells, Addenda
Series XIX: Oversize

University of Chicago Library

Guide to the Ida B. Wells Papers 1884-1976

© 2009 University of Chicago Library

Descriptive Summary

Title: Wells, Ida B. Papers
Dates: 1884-1976
Size: 6 linear feet (11 boxes)
Repository: Special Collections Research Center, University of Chicago Library, 1100 East 57th Street, Chicago, Illinois 60637 U.S.A.
Abstract: Ida B. Wells, (1862-1931) teacher, journalist and anti-lynching activist. Paper contain correspondence, manuscript of Crusade for Justice: the Autobiography of Ida B. Wells, diaries, copies of articles and speeches by Wells, articles and accounts about Wells, newspapers clippings, and photographs. Also contains Alfreda M. Duster's (Wells' daughter) working copies of the autobiography which Duster edited. Correspondents include Frederick Douglass and Albion Tourgee. Includes photocopies of correspondence of Wells' husband Ferdinand Barnett and a scrapbook of newspapers articles written by him.

Information on Use

Access

The collection is open for research. A scrapbook, located in Series XVIII, Subseries 1, by Ferdinand Barnett is restricted due to its fragile condition. A photocopy has been produced for researchers and is located in a binder in Box 10.

Digital Images

Original documents, texts, and images represented by digital images linked to this finding aid are subject to U. S. copyright law. It is the user's sole responsibility to secure any necessary copyright permission to reproduce or publish documents, texts, and images from any holders of rights in the original materials.

The University of Chicago Library, in its capacity as owner of the physical property represented by the digital images linked to this finding aid, encourages the use of these materials for educational and scholarly purposes. Any reproduction or publication from these digital images requires that the following credit line be included: Special Collections Research Center, University of Chicago Library.

The images presented here may include materials reflecting the attitudes, language, and stereotypes of an earlier time period. These materials are presented as historical resources in support of study and research. Inclusion of such materials does not constitute an endorsement of their content by the University of Chicago.

The University of Chicago Library appreciates hearing from anyone who may have information about any of the images in this collection.

Citation

When quoting material from this collection, the preferred citation is: Wells, Ida B. Papers, [Box #, Folder #], Special Collections Research Center, University of Chicago Library

Biographical Note

Ida B. Wells was born in Holly Springs, Mississippi in 1862, six months before the Emancipation Proclamation granted freedom to her slave parents. Following the death of both her parents of yellow fever in 1878, Ida, at age 16, began teaching in a one-room schoolhouse in rural Mississippi. Some time between 1882 and 1883 Wells moved to Memphis, Tennessee, to teach in city schools. She was dismissed, in 1891, for her outspoken criticism of segregated schools.

Her dismissal from the Memphis school system would be the beginning of her protests about justice, particularly as they pertained to the treatment of black Americans. In 1884 Ida B. Wells sued the Chesapeake & Ohio Railroad for forcing blacks to ride in segregated and inferior carriages. Ida B. Wells won this case in the local court, but was defeated in the Supreme Court. Undaunted by heavy opposition and a seemingly hopeless cause, however, Wells, from that point on, made the welfare of African American people her main concern, meeting every obstacle head on with a characteristic determination.

Proceedings of the National Negro Conference 1909 *is a printed collection of the talks from the event. It includes a transcript of Ida B. Wells's speech. This historical document also reveals the spellings, language, and customs that were common at the time.*

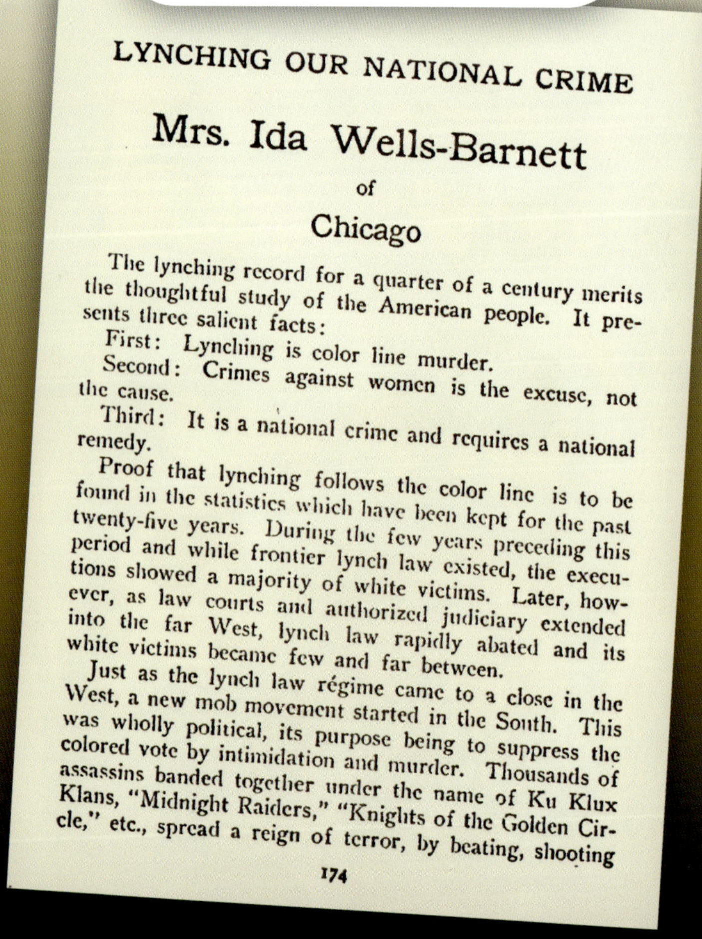

LYNCHING OUR NATIONAL CRIME

Mrs. Ida Wells-Barnett

of

Chicago

The lynching record for a quarter of a century merits the thoughtful study of the American people. It presents three salient facts:

First: Lynching is color line murder.

Second: Crimes against women is the excuse, not the cause.

Third: It is a national crime and requires a national remedy.

Proof that lynching follows the color line is to be found in the statistics which have been kept for the past twenty-five years. During the few years preceding this period and while frontier lynch law existed, the executions showed a majority of white victims. Later, however, as law courts and authorized judiciary extended into the far West, lynch law rapidly abated and its white victims became few and far between.

Just as the lynch law régime came to a close in the West, a new mob movement started in the South. This was wholly political, its purpose being to suppress the colored vote by intimidation and murder. Thousands of assassins banded together under the name of Ku Klux Klans, "Midnight Raiders," "Knights of the Golden Circle," etc., spread a reign of terror, by beating, shooting

174

BEHIND THE WORDS

Social worker Lillian Wald founded the Henry Street Settlement in 1893. The community center aimed to help poor families in the neighborhood. The National Negro Conference also wanted to help people, but its focus was country wide. Many of the key figures at the event helped create the NAACP that year. Wells was one of the founders of the NAACP. She left the group because she felt it was not taking enough action. Wells was known for not being afraid to voice her opinion.

Speaker: *Ida B. Wells-Barnett*
Audience: *National Negro Conference*
Date: *June 1, 1909*

"***...an influential body of citizens...***

It is a national crime and requires a national remedy.

Lynching is color line murder...Crimes against women is the excuse, not the cause."

Wells described the attendees of the conference

Argued that America must treat lynching as a crime to end it

Wells's point of view was that racists used lynching as a way to control African Americans

William Edward Burghardt Du Bois was a ***notable*** *civil rights activist who also spoke at the conference.*

Lillian Wald believed everyone was entitled to equal and fair health care regardless of their socio-economic status, race, gender, or age. She founded the Henry Street Settlement in New York City.

William English Walling was an organizer of the conference and a founder of the NAACP.

CHANGE MAKERS

People use the spoken word to help push for change. Speeches are crafted to sway an audience to think a certain way. Ida B. Wells tried to raise awareness and gain support to end lynching. She relied on a few common features that are found in most **persuasive** speeches.

Speechwriters take great care to choose just the right words to make an argument.

MAKING AN ARGUMENT

CLAIM

Speeches support their arguments with claims, which are statements or conclusions.

Schools discriminate when they order students to change their hairstyles.

EVIDENCE

Evidence is data or facts that prove the claims are true.

Hairstyles worn by African Americans are the ones most likely to be singled out in a school setting.

WARRANT

Warrants connect evidence and claims to support a course of action.

If a school's rules are based on what one group views as acceptable, they must be reconsidered.

APPEAL

Appeals in speeches urge the audience to act.

Demand that schools treat all students with fairness!

INFLUENCING THE AUDIENCE

Rhetoric is the art of **persuasion** used in speeches and many other texts. Rhetorical language uses three main ways to convince the audience.

LOGOS

Logos asks the audience to consider logic, or reason. In a speech, logos may begin with a general idea that is supported by facts. It could also use these facts as a starting point and draw conclusions.

Students from all backgrounds should be treated with respect. Judging one group based on how they look is discrimination.

ETHOS

Ethos urges the audience to believe the speaker because of his or her good character. This may be done by sharing personal experiences, finding common ground, or showing respect.

We all want our children to feel welcome, safe, and included.

PATHOS

Pathos plays on the audience's emotions to win them over.

Imagine a little girl being told that she cannot go to school because of her beautiful braids. Would you want a friend to be treated like that?

Anyone can use rhetorical language to strengthen the claims, evidence, and warrants in their speeches.

DIGGING DEEPER

Do you think someone could make a persuasive speech without knowing anything about rhetoric? Why or why not?

WORDS THAT WORK

Speakers use rhetorical language in different ways. They may also use rhetorical devices, such as:

- Figurative language, such as **metaphors** and **similes**
- Comparing two unalike things in an **analogy**
- Repeating key words and phrases
- Exaggerating in **hyperboles**
- Giving things human qualities through **personification**
- Making some facts sound less important than they are.

HEARD NOT READ

Reading a speech silently is not the same experience as hearing it. Language and voice add power to a spoken argument. The ways a speaker uses his or her voice can change how the same words are heard. How someone pronounces and produces the sounds in words is called diction. It also includes the words a speaker or writer chooses to use. The **tone** used can also alter the message. Cadence is the rising and falling rhythms of those tones. Along with emphasis, all these things help speakers make their points.

IDA'S VOICE

About nine out of ten enslaved people in the United States could not read or write. Slave owners denied them the chance to learn. The Wells family valued education. James Wells, Ida's father, helped found Shaw University after the Civil War. It educated formerly enslaved people. Ida was a student there. Her level of education was clear in her speech writing. There are no recordings of Wells's speeches to study. Little is known about her speaking style. However, she was known to be intelligent and fierce. The lack of descriptions in secondary sources may reveal **systemic** racist and sexist beliefs. African Americans and women were seen as less important. Wells stood up for herself and others against this discrimination.

DIGGING DEEPER

If there are no recordings of a speech, it is impossible to know for sure how the speaker delivered it. How might have Ida B. Wells used her voice to sway the audience?

Ida studied at Shaw University, Mississippi, now known as Rust College.

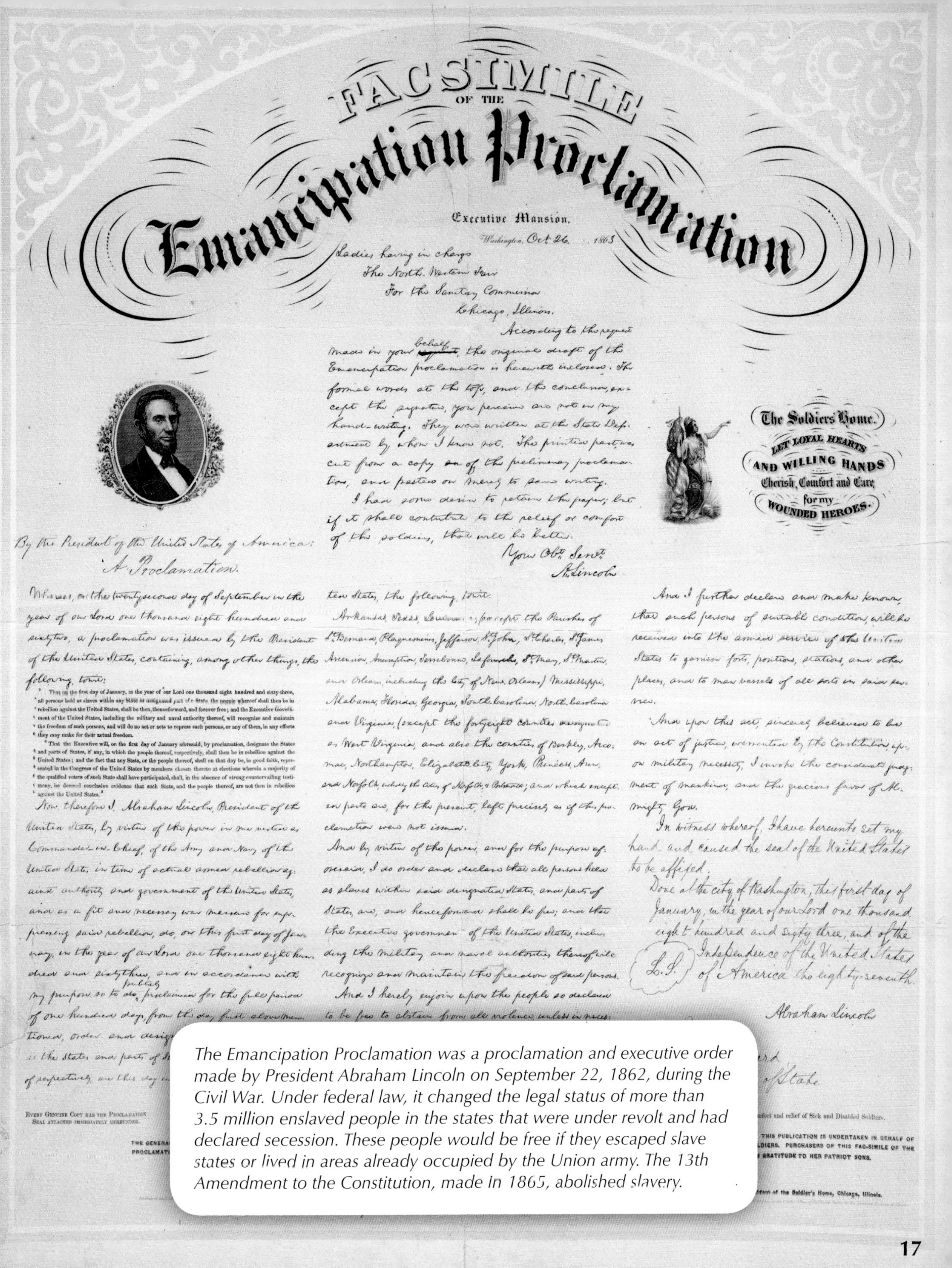

The Emancipation Proclamation was a proclamation and executive order made by President Abraham Lincoln on September 22, 1862, during the Civil War. Under federal law, it changed the legal status of more than 3.5 million enslaved people in the states that were under revolt and had declared secession. These people would be free if they escaped slave states or lived in areas already occupied by the Union army. The 13th Amendment to the Constitution, made in 1865, abolished slavery.

CHAPTER 2

WORDS AND MEANING

Deconstructing a speech means taking it apart. Reading the whole speech is the first step. If possible, listen to it too. Look at how the speaker presents information. Find the parts of his or her argument. Watch for the rhetorical language described in the last chapter. This will show how the speaker felt about the issue. Deconstructing Ida B. Wells's speech reveals her many years of in-depth research. She showed why she believed lynching was a crime and why she wanted the American government to treat it that way.

PRESENTING IDEAS

Speakers present their ideas in a variety of ways. Placing them in order is called sequencing. For example, "Lynching, Our National Crime" begins by listing three related facts. Wells even numbered them for emphasis. She also used the comparative style. This relies on comparison and contrast. One way Wells used this style was by comparing the 959 lynching victims from the previous decade. Just over 100 of them were white, whereas 857 were African Americans. These numbers proved her argument that lynching was a race issue. Speeches may also arrange ideas casually. This style considers causes and effects.

Sequencing

> *The lynching record for a quarter of a century merits the thoughtful study of the American people. It presents three salient facts:*
>
> *First: Lynching is color line murder.*
>
> *Second: Crimes against women is the excuse, not the cause.*
>
> *Third: It is a national crime and requires a national remedy.*

Comparative style

> *During the last ten years from 1899 to 1908 inclusive the number lynched was 959. Of this number 102 were white while the colored victims numbered 857.*

PURPOSE

The purpose of a speech is the reason for making it. Ida B. Wells wanted people to understand the real reasons behind lynching. It was a way for white people to hold onto their power. Her goal was to argue that it was a crime that needed to be stopped by the government of the United States.

DECONSTRUCT IT

To determine the purpose of a speech, listen to it or read it and ask:

- What is the speaker's central argument?
- Who is the speaker trying to appeal to?

Speaker: *Ida B. Wells-Barnett*
Audience: *National Negro Conference*
Date: *June 1, 1909*

"*Upon the **grave** question presented by the **slaughter** of innocent men, women and children there should be an honest, **courageous conference of patriotic, law-abiding citizens** anxious to punish crime promptly, **impartially and by due process of law**, also to make **life, liberty, and property** secure against **mob rule**.*"

- **grave**: Means "serious" and suggests death
- **slaughter**: Term often connected with the killing of animals, which is how some African Americans were treated
- **courageous conference of patriotic, law-abiding citizens**: Appealed to brave, united Americans
- **impartially and by due process of law**: Fairness and legality contrast with lynching itself
- **life, liberty, and property**: Philosopher John Locke wrote about these rights in 1689 and the Declaration of Independence echoed them
- **mob rule**: Control by groups outside of the law

The earliest attempt to pass a U.S. House of Representatives anti-lynching bill was in 1900. The Emmett Till Anti Lynching Act was approved by the House in February 2020. It was named after a 14-year-old boy who was killed in Mississippi in 1955.

SPEAKER SPOTLIGHT

Ida B. Wells wrote many newspaper articles about lynching. Their purpose was to inform Americans and **condemn** the killings. On June 25, 1892, *The New York Age* ran her piece called "Exiled." In it, Wells described the events that led to a mob attacking her *Memphis Free Speech* office. She also explained why she kept up the fight against lynching. Wells argued, "Somebody must show that the Afro-American race is more sinned against than sinning, and it seems to have fallen upon me to do so. The awful death-roll…is appalling…" Women's groups in New York and Brooklyn paid to print the article as a pamphlet later that year.

Wells's investigative skills presented evidence that lynchings were a deadly tool used to stifle and punish Black economic progress.

SOUTHERN HORRORS.
LYNCH LAW
IN ALL
ITS PHASES

IDA B. WELLS.

Fifteen C

THE NEW YORK AGE PRIN
1892.

READ IT

"Southern Horrors: Lynch Law In All Its Phases" was published as a pamphlet in 1892. Read the full text here: **https://bit.ly/2V7H4Tm**

LYNCH LAW IN THE UNITED STATES.
To the EDITOR *of the* DAILY POST.

Sir,—"A City Councillor" asks in Saturday's *Post*, "What possible practical object can be attained by such meetings?" He refers to the meeting to be held Wednesday, in which an exposition of lynch law in the Southern States of America will be given by the writer. I beg space to answer that question. Resentment because of the freedom and citizenship of the negro race has been continually shown by southern whites. In the ten years succeeding the civil war thousands of negroes were murdered for the crime (?) of casting the ballot, and their vote is entirely nullified throughout the entire South. The laws of the Southern States make it a crime for whites and negroes to intermarry, or even ride in the same railway carriage. Both crimes (?) are punishable by fine and imprisonment. The doors of the churches, hotels, concert-halls, and reading-rooms are alike closed against the negro as a man, but every place is open to him as a servant.

The latest culmination of this war against negro progress is the substitution of mob rule for courts of justice throughout the South. The judges, juries, sheriffs, and gaolers in these States are all white men, and thus make it impossible for a negro to escape the penalty for any crime he commits. Yet wherever a black man is charged with crime against a white person, these mobs, without disguise, take him from the gaols in broad daylight, and hang, shoot, stab, or burn him to death, as their fancy dictates. A coroner's jury renders a verdict that "the deceased came to his death at the hands of parties unknown to the jury." In the past ten years, over one thousand black men, women, and children have met this violent death at the hands of white mobs. And the rest of America has remained silent; not even when three men were burned alive in the past twelve months, has she opened her mouth to protest against this barbarism. One religious body which met in Philadelphia last June refused to pass a resolution condemning lynching because it feared to offend the Southern delegates present.

The pulpit and press of our own country remain silent on these continued outrages; the voice of my race, thus tortured and outraged, wherever lifted in America in a demand for justice is stifled or ignored. It is to the religious and moral sentiment of Great Britain we turn. These can arouse the public sentiment of America so necessary for the enforcement of law. The moral agencies at work in Great Britain did much for the final overthrow of chattel slavery. They can, in like manner, pray and write and preach and talk and act against civil and industrial slavery; against the hanging, shooting, and burning alive of a powerless race. America cannot and will not ignore the voice of a nation that is her superior in civilisation, which makes this demand in the name of justice and humanity. If the moral reforms of the age have been brought about by Christianity, here is one which calls loudly for Christian and moral effort. I am in Great Britain today because I believe that the silent indifference with ...ed the intelligence that human ... in a Christian (?) country and ...axon communities is born of ...ation; and that if she really ...he protest long and loud. The ... with which my story has been ...nd England, the prompt and ...f protest and condemnation of ...d me of the truth of my suppos... ...he people of Birmingham, when ...ill not be one whit less willing, ...eir moral influence to check wha... ...onal evil.

IDA B. WELLS,
Of Memphis, Tennessee, U.S.A.
66, Gough Road, Birmingham, May 14.

Wells went to Britain on two lecture tours and wrote columns in British papers. She hoped to gather support from outside the country that would lead to shaming and anti-lynching laws inside the country.

New York Age-Feb.18,1893

THE REIGN OF MOB LAW
Iola's Opinion of Doings in the Southern Fiel...

The lynchiing epidemic still rages in Texas. Gov. Hogg denounced the ly...
who burned Henry Smith as murderers, telegraphed the District Attorney a...
sheriff of Lamar County, where the burning occurred", to discharge their d...
and amke complaint and report those known to have been engaged in the
lynching" ... The mob has so little fear and so great contempt of the Gov-
ernor, the sheriff and the District Attorney that it went a few days later
February 7th and lynched Will Butler.
Will Butler was a stepson of Henry Smith, the man who was burned alive, and
made himself notorous during the search for Smith by claiming to know his
whereabouts which he would not divulge" -- so said the dispatches. Hence,
because Will Butler did not tell where his step-father was, he too was
lynched. ...
New Orleans, Jan. 21- A mob of masked men broke into the jail last night at
Convent, St. Joseph Parish and forced the jailer to open the cells of Robert
Landy and Pick George, who were incarcerated there, one for garroting and rob-
bing a telegraph operator at Dehon Station and the other for murdering a
man named Denhorst.
... and lynched. Our race still sits and does nothing

DIGGING DEEPER

Do you think everyone is treated equally in today's society? Why or why not?

CLAIMS AND EVIDENCE

Speeches back their arguments with claims and evidence. The audience, time period, and setting influence what a speaker includes. One of the claims that Ida B. Wells made was that **white supremacist** groups kept African Americans from making political change. Black men had been guaranteed the right to vote in 1870. However, some Southerners fought against this new nation-wide equality. Wells cited dates, cases, methods used to murder victims, and geographical trends to prove her claim.

*The 15th Amendment to the U.S. Constitution gave Black men the right to vote. Southern states did their best to stop them for another 100 years. Women could vote after the 19th Amendment was adopted in 1920. Black women were mostly prevented from voting through **discriminatory** state practices until the passage of the Voting Rights Act in 1965.*

The Ku Klux Klan is one of the American hate groups Ida B. Wells mentioned in her speech.

DECONSTRUCT IT

To find claims and evidence in a speech, ask:

- What conclusions are being made?
- Which facts or data support these statements?
- Does the speaker use voice, such as emphasis or pacing, to reinforce any text?

By the end of the Civil War 10 percent of the Union troops, or 179,000 men were African American. Another 19,000 served in the navy and over 40,000 died.

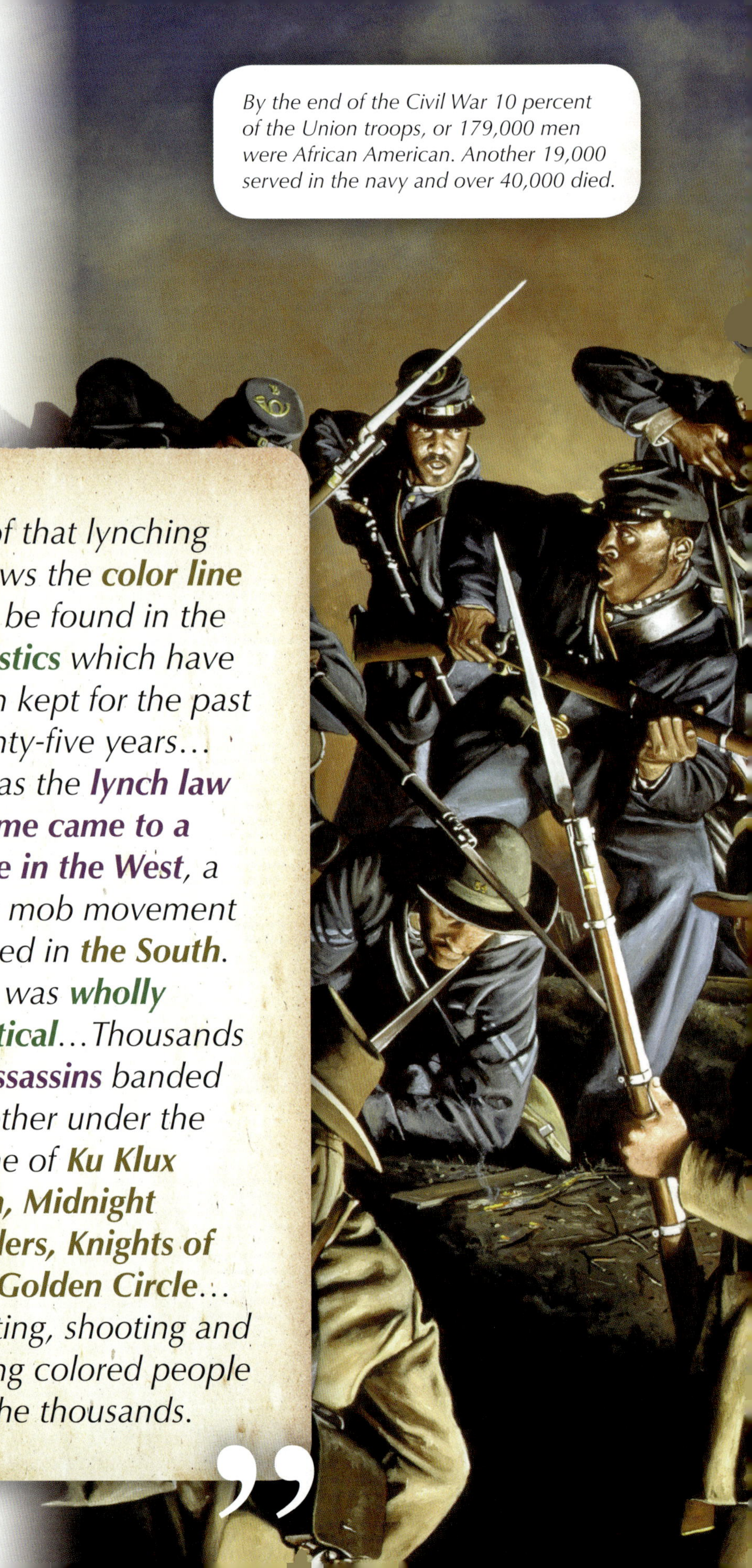

Speaker: *Ida B. Wells-Barnett*
Audience: *National Negro Conference*
Date: *June 1, 1909*

*"Proof that lynching follows the **color line** is to be found in the **statistics** which have been kept for the past twenty-five years... Just as the **lynch law regime came to a close in the West**, a new mob movement started in **the South**. This was **wholly political**...Thousands of **assassins** banded together under the name of **Ku Klux Klan, Midnight Raiders, Knights of the Golden Circle**... beating, shooting and killing colored people by the thousands."*

Based on race

Measurable data

Lynching ended in western states as they formed legal systems

Included Georgia, Mississippi, Texas, and other southern states

Lynching scared African Americans away from voting

Murderers

These groups believed white people were superior to other races

BEHIND THE WORDS

At first, lynching was more common in the western states. It was a simple way to punish anyone in unsettled areas. Lynching became rare in the West as its legal systems improved. The southern version focused on controlling African Americans. The **Confederate army** had fought to keep slavery in the United States. It had been less than 45 years since the Confederate states lost the Civil War. Intimidation and violence helped white people in the South hold onto their power.

Ida B. Wells also fought for American women's right to vote. She formed the Alpha Suffrage Club in Chicago in 1913 to press for voting rights for all women.

SPEAKER SPOTLIGHT

Ida B. Wells spoke out about lynching for over a decade before the National Negro Conference. One of her most famous speeches is "Lynch Law in America." She delivered it in Chicago, Illinois. The claims in this address from 1900 are similar to those in her conference speech. She argued, "Our country's national crime is lynching." This was murder by "intelligent people" who put "human beings to death…without trial by jury, without opportunity to make defense, and without right of appeal." This was clearly outside of the law.

The lynching of Henry Smith in Paris, Texas, on February 3, 1893, was a public spectacle that 15,000 people gathered to watch. Smith was accused of murdering a child. Ida investigated the lynching. She determined Smith may have committed murder but the vicious details of the crime had been made up by his accusers in order to torture and kill him without trial.

READ IT

Read the full text of "Lynch Law in America": **https://bit.ly/2zzDxWa**

WARRANTS AND APPEALS

Appeals in speeches request action of some kind. Warrants are statements that support this course of action. Ida B. Wells connected the claims and evidence in warrants to convince the audience that lynching was murder. She appealed to the attendees of the conference and the rest of the country to protect everyone from this crime.

DECONSTRUCT IT

Find warrants and appeals in a speech by asking:

- Is the speaker urging the audience to act or think a certain way?
- How are claims and evidence being connected to convince them?

Speaker: *Ida B. Wells-Barnett*
Audience: *National Negro Conference*
Date: *June 1, 1909*

> *The only certain* ***remedy*** *is an* ***appeal to law****. Lawbreakers must be made to know that human life is* ***sacred****...* ***The strong arm of the government*** *must reach across state lines whenever* ***unbridled lawlessness defies state laws*** *and must give to the individual citizen under the* ***Stars and Stripes*** *the same measure of protection which it gives to him when he travels in foreign land.*

- **Solution**
- **To make lynching a crime**
- **Valued and respected**
- **The power of the federal government**
- **Lynching went unchecked even if it was against the law in some states**
- **American flag**

BEHIND THE WORDS

The country struggled to unite the northern and southern states. Each one had its own way of doing things. What was legal in one state might not be legal in another. Ida B. Wells wanted the national government to take control. She suggested that African Americans were less safe in the United States than if they left the country. The U.S. would fight for them if they faced violence elsewhere. At home, they might be lynched with no consequences.

The American flag is called the Stars and Stripes because of its design.

RHETORICAL LANGUAGE

Speeches use rhetorical language, including logos, ethos, and pathos, to make claims, support them with evidence, and make appeals and warrants. Ida B. Wells depended strongly on logic and reason. Her argument was well researched and backed up with facts. They helped her draw conclusions. They also helped her build **credibility** with her audience. The real-life examples of lynching that she described played on their emotions as a persuasive strategy.

DECONSTRUCT IT

To identify the rhetorical language in a speech, ask:

- How is the speaker using logic and reason to persuade the audience?
- Does the speaker's character help support the central argument?
- How is the audience being swayed by emotion?

> *...3,284 men,* ***women and children*** *have been* ***put to death****...the irresponsible* ***blood-thirsty criminals who swept through the streets of Springfield****, beating* ***an inoffensive law-abiding citizen*** *to death in one part of the town, and in another torturing and shooting to death* ***a man*** *who, for* ***threescore*** *years,* ***had made a reputation for honesty, integrity and sobriety,*** *had raised a family and had accumulated property, was not* ***deterred****...*

Repeated three times that this affected more than Black men, who were often accused of violence against white women

The reality of what lynching was

Mob presented as the wrongdoers

As described in the Introduction

Scott Burton, an innocent African American

William Donnegan, see pages 4 and 5

Sixty

Donnegan was known to be trustworthy and thoughtful

Stopped

Speaker: *Ida B. Wells-Barnett*
Audience: *National Negro Conference*
Date: *June 1, 1909*

BEHIND THE WORDS

Ida B. Wells described the victims of lynching as average American citizens. She saw the mob who punished them outside the law as the criminals. Wells noted that even women and children were being burned alive. Her argument gained credibility when she described two of the victims from the lynchings in Springfield, Illinois. These men were not the kind of person who most Americans thought were being lynched. They were murdered because of resentments felt by their fellow citizens who were white.

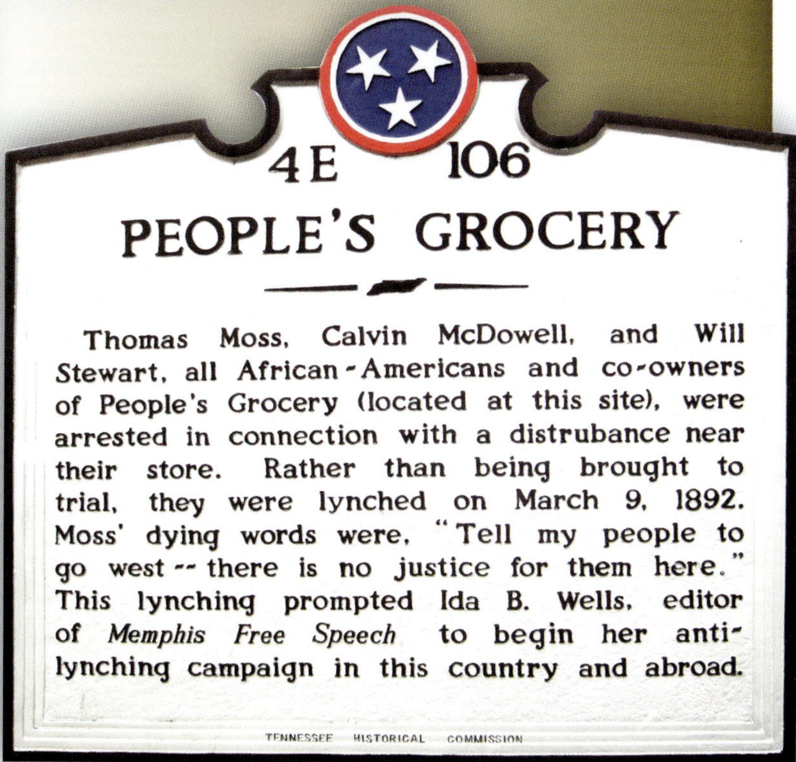

Ida B. Wells (left) with Thomas Moss's wife Betty and her children Maurine and Thomas.

SPEAKER SPOTLIGHT

"Lynch Law in All Its Phases" is another of Ida B. Wells's popular speeches. She delivered it at the Tremont Temple in Boston on February 13, 1893. The audience was mainly white. This was a new experience for Wells. She drew on logos, ethos, and pathos to connect with them. Wells focused on the lynching of her friend Thomas Moss. She included many details and facts. Sharing her personal experience with lynching helped her gain trust. She used pathos as she described Moss's family: "The baby daughter of Tom Moss, too young to express how she misses her father…stretches up her little hands to be taken up into the arms which will nevermore clasp his daughter's form. His wife holds Thomas Moss, Jr., in her arms…the tears fall thick and fast when she is thinking of the sad fate of the father he will never see, and of the two helpless children who cling to her for the support she cannot give."

READ IT

To read the whole "Lynch Law in All Its Phases" speech, visit: **https://bit.ly/3czCxj8**

DIGGING DEEPER

The lack of recordings can make it difficult to prove what was really said in a speech. Printed transcripts can alter the wording. What problems could this pose?

CHAPTER 3

ANALYZING PERSPECTIVES

Sometimes, one person writes a speech and someone else delivers it. The writer must try to present the speaker's perspective, or point of view. Ida B. Wells wrote her own speeches. "Lynching, Our National Crime" revealed that she thought lynching was a crime. The attendees at the National Negro Conference likely agreed. However, Wells's speech makes it clear that some Americans had different perspectives on lynching in 1909.

DIGGING DEEPER

Do you think it is helpful for a speechwriter and a speaker to have the same point of view? Why or why not?

A MOMENT IN TIME

Both the maker and the audience are products of their time. Ida B. Wells was born into slavery during the American Civil War. She was very young when the war and slavery ended. Inequality and discrimination did not stop in 1865, however. Wells experienced both throughout her life. Her view that lynching was race-based murder came from personal experience and careful research. The group that gathered at the Henry Street Settlement House shared her goal to help African Americans. Given the time period, it is not surprising that they met in a northern state. People from the South were less likely to be found at this kind of event in the early 1900s.

In 1867, Black men voted for the first time.

EARLY INFLUENCES

When Ida B. Wells was 16, her parents and baby brother died of yellow fever. She had to leave school to support her younger siblings. Wells lied about her age to become a teacher. In 1882, the family moved to live with an aunt in Memphis, Tennessee. Wells taught at a **segregated** school there. She was fired after publicly criticizing and writing about its poor conditions. Wells never backed down, though. When she was 20, a train conductor ordered her to move from a first-class car to a lower-class one. He was separating African Americans from the white people on the train. When Wells refused to move, she was forced off at the next station. She sued and won. However, her victory was overturned by the Tennessee Supreme Court. These experiences all helped lead to Wells becoming a civil rights activist.

Ida B. Wells refused to give up her train seat for white passengers in 1883—72 years before Rosa Parks did the same thing on a bus.

The 14th Amendment to the Constitution was ratified on July 9, 1868. It granted citizenship to "all persons born or naturalized in the United States." This included formerly enslaved people. The 15th Amendment, in 1869, gave Black men the right to vote. Between 1873 and 1883, the Supreme Court issued a series of decisions that set back federal government efforts to protect the civil rights of African Americans. These lasted until 1957. Between 1890 and 1910, most former Confederate states amended their constitutions to legalize the **disenfranchisement** of African Americans. These were known as the Jim Crow laws. At the same time, lynchings were used as a tool to reinforce white supremacy.

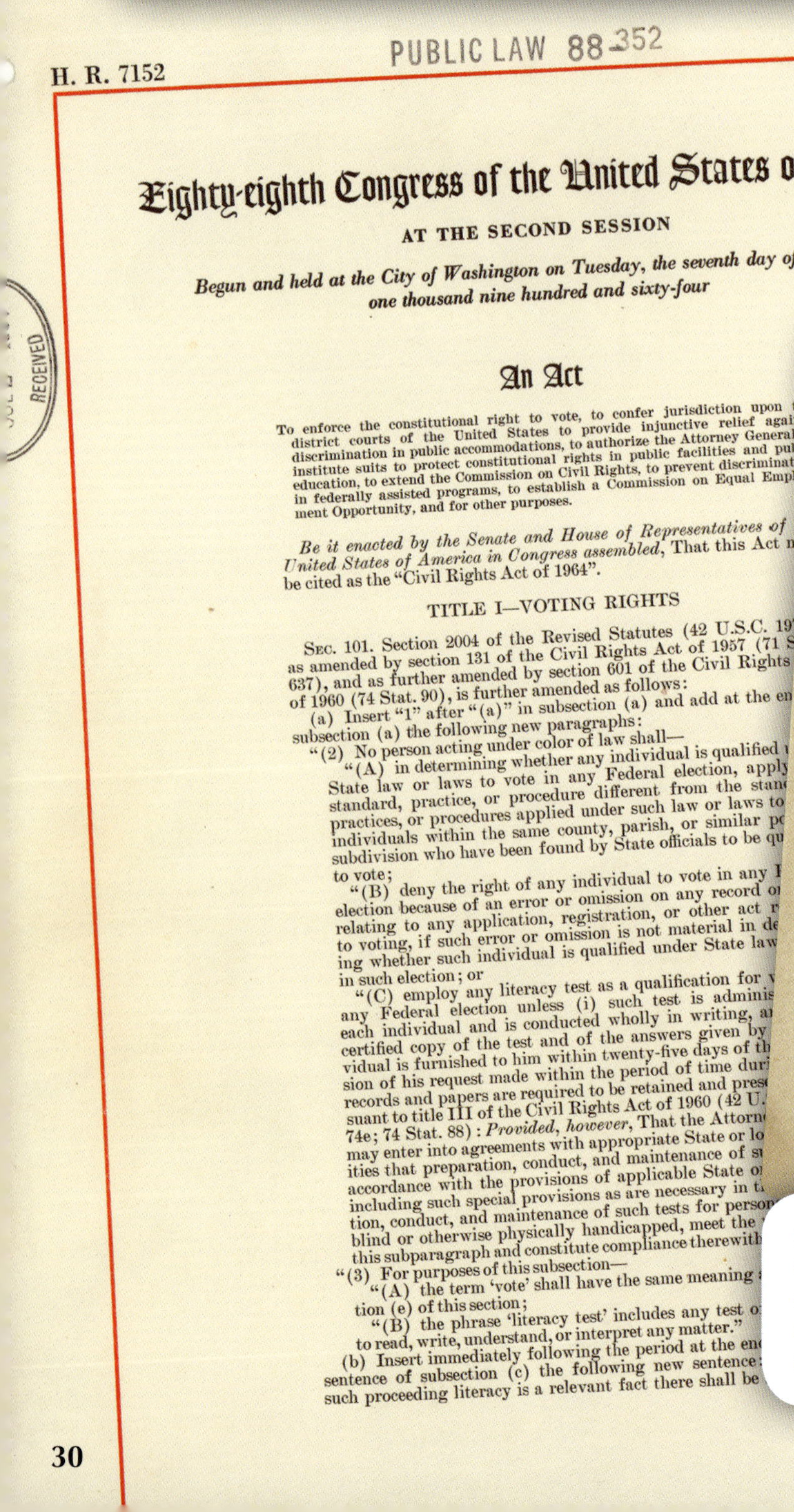
PUBLIC LAW 88-352

H. R. 7152

Eighty-eighth Congress of the United States of America

AT THE SECOND SESSION

Begun and held at the City of Washington on Tuesday, the seventh day of January, one thousand nine hundred and sixty-four

An Act

To enforce the constitutional right to vote, to confer jurisdiction upon the district courts of the United States to provide injunctive relief against discrimination in public accommodations, to authorize the Attorney General to institute suits to protect constitutional rights in public facilities and public education, to extend the Commission on Civil Rights, to prevent discrimination in federally assisted programs, to establish a Commission on Equal Employment Opportunity, and for other purposes.

Be it enacted by the Senate and House of Representatives of the United States of America in Congress assembled, That this Act may be cited as the "Civil Rights Act of 1964".

TITLE I—VOTING RIGHTS

SEC. 101. Section 2004 of the Revised Statutes (42 U.S.C. 197... as amended by section 131 of the Civil Rights Act of 1957 (71 S... 637), and as further amended by section 601 of the Civil Rights... of 1960 (74 Stat. 90), is further amended as follows:

(a) Insert "1" after "(a)" in subsection (a) and add at the en... subsection (a) the following new paragraphs:

"(2) No person acting under color of law shall—

"(A) in determining whether any individual is qualified ... State law or laws to vote in any Federal election, apply... standard, practice, or procedure different from the stan... practices, or procedures applied under such law or laws to... individuals within the same county, parish, or similar p... subdivision who have been found by State officials to be qu... to vote;

"(B) deny the right of any individual to vote in any F... election because of an error or omission on any record o... relating to any application, registration, or other act r... to voting, if such error or omission is not material in de... ing whether such individual is qualified under State law... in such election; or

"(C) employ any literacy test as a qualification for v... any Federal election unless (i) such test is adminis... each individual and is conducted wholly in writing, a... certified copy of the test and of the answers given by... vidual is furnished to him within twenty-five days of th... sion of his request made within the period of time dur... records and papers are required to be retained and pres... suant to title III of the Civil Rights Act of 1960 (42 U... 74e; 74 Stat. 88): *Provided, however,* That the Attorn... may enter into agreements with appropriate State or lo... ities that preparation, conduct, and maintenance of s... accordance with the provisions of applicable State o... including such special provisions as are necessary in t... tion, conduct, and maintenance of such tests for person... blind or otherwise physically handicapped, meet the ... this subparagraph and constitute compliance therewith...

"(3) For purposes of this subsection—

"(A) the term 'vote' shall have the same meaning ... tion (e) of this section;

"(B) the phrase 'literacy test' includes any test o... to read, write, understand, or interpret any matter."

(b) Insert immediately following the period at the en... sentence of subsection (c) the following new sentence: ... such proceeding literacy is a relevant fact there shall be...

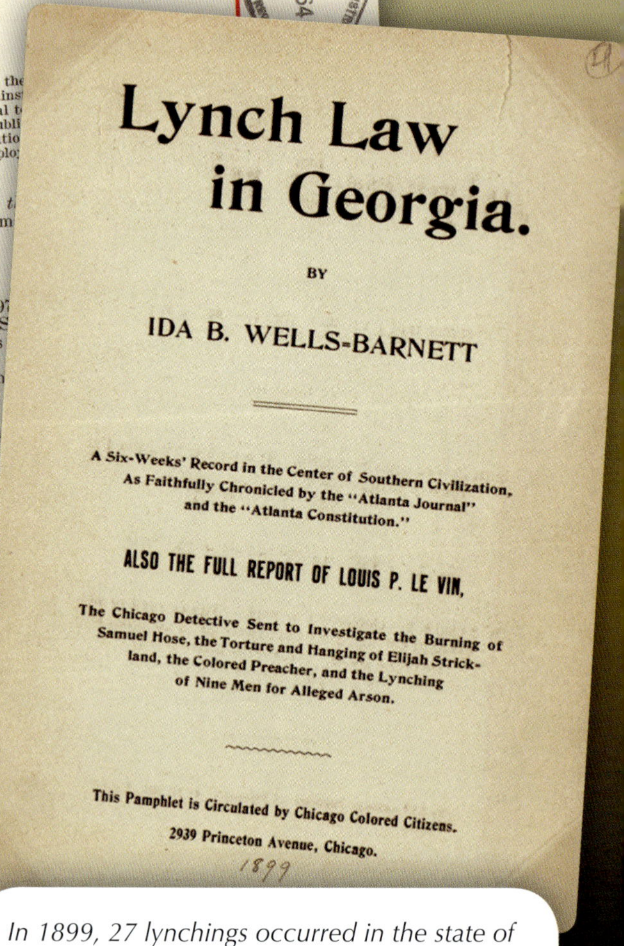
Lynch Law in Georgia.

BY

IDA B. WELLS-BARNETT

A Six-Weeks' Record in the Center of Southern Civilization, As Faithfully Chronicled by the "Atlanta Journal" and the "Atlanta Constitution."

ALSO THE FULL REPORT OF LOUIS P. LE VIN,

The Chicago Detective Sent to Investigate the Burning of Samuel Hose, the Torture and Hanging of Elijah Strickland, the Colored Preacher, and the Lynching of Nine Men for Alleged Arson.

This Pamphlet is Circulated by Chicago Colored Citizens.

2939 Princeton Avenue, Chicago.

1899

In 1899, 27 lynchings occurred in the state of Georgia alone. Ida helped hire a white private detective, Louis P. Le Vin, to investigate several lynchings. She then reprinted his report with other material as "Lynch Law in Georgia."

On September 22 to 24, 1906, an armed mob of white people attacked African Americans in Atlanta, lynching several and killing at least 25. The attack is known as the Atlanta Massacre of 1906.

SPEAKER SPOTLIGHT

Ida B. Wells began writing a book about her life when she was in her sixties. She did not finish it before she died. Her daughter, Alfreda Duster, completed the book. *Crusade for Justice: The Autobiography of Ida B. Wells* was published in 1970. It described the incident on the train. The book tells Wells's side of the story. This passage shows the opposing perspectives at that time: "He tried to drag me out of the seat, but the moment he caught hold of my arm I fastened my teeth in the back of his hand. I had braced my feet against the seat in front and was holding onto the back... He...got the baggageman and another man to help him...They were encouraged to do this by the attitude of the white ladies and gentlemen in the car; some of them even stood on seats so that they could get a good view and continued applauding..."

Alfreda Duster (bottom) was one of Ida B. Wells's four children.

WELL-CHOSEN WORDS

Nuanced language uses certain words to create a feeling that sways the audience. These word choices also reveal the speechmaker's perspective. Wells described lynching as "mob murder" three times in her speech. This showed her point of view that lynching was unlawful. Loaded language is meant to stir up the audience's emotions. For example, Wells said, "...only under the Stars and Stripes is the human holocaust possible." This brought to mind the American flag and called upon the listeners' patriotism. The term "holocaust" refers to complete destruction. Using it highlighted the huge impact of the murders.

DECONSTRUCT IT

To examine a speaker's perspective, ask:

- How does the language used show the speaker's feelings?
- How could the speaker's point of view be summed up in one sentence?

Speaker: *Ida B. Wells-Barnett*
Audience: *National Negro Conference*
Date: *June 1, 1909*

"*In a few years, **the purpose was accomplished** and **the black vote was suppressed**...**Mob murder** increased yearly until in 1892 more than 200 victims were lynched and statistics show that 3,284 men, women and children have been put to death in this **quarter of a century**... What is the cause of this awful slaughter? This question is answered almost daily—**always the same shameless falsehood that Negroes are lynched to protect womanhood**.*"

Intimidating African Americans

They were discouraged from voting for their own interests

Loaded language to describe lynching

25 years

Wells's point of view was that this was just an excuse to murder people

SPEAKER SPOTLIGHT

Ida B. Wells believed lynchers wanted to intimidate African Americans. In *Crusade for Justice: The Autobiography of Ida B. Wells*, she described how she felt about the mob trying to scare her into giving up her fight. "I felt that one had better die fighting against injustice than to die like a dog or a rat in a trap. I had already determined to sell my life as dearly as possible if attacked. I felt if I could take one lyncher with me, this would even up the score a little bit." Wells intended to fight back if someone tried to lynch her. She saw her battle as necessary, even if her life was at risk.

LIMITED VIEW

Most speeches and other primary sources present a single perspective about an issue. A maker may leave out facts that do not support his or her view. This may limit what can be learned from them. Ida B. Wells gave some space in her speech to another point of view when she quoted John Temple Graves. He was in favor of lynching. Wells did not agree that Graves was correct. Instead, she argued, "All know that it is untrue." She claimed that the data proved that lynchers knew they were **hypocrites**.

DECONSTRUCT IT

To find the limitations of a speech, ask:

- How does the maker's perspective shape this primary source?
- Are any important facts being left out?
- Based on evidence from other sources, are there any points that should be explored further?

Speaker: *Ida B. Wells-Barnett, in response to John Temple Graves*
Audience: *National Negro Conference*
Date: *June 1, 1909*

> *The cowardly lyncher **revels** in murder, then seeks to shield himself from **public execration** by **claiming devotion to woman**. But truth is mighty and the lynching record **discloses the hypocrisy** of the lyncher as well as his crime.*

Celebrates and enjoys

Being judged by other citizens for bad behavior

Protecting women from rape was an excuse

Makes the double-standards known

John Temple Graves wrote for newspapers, just like Ida B. Wells did. Their perspectives were very different, however.

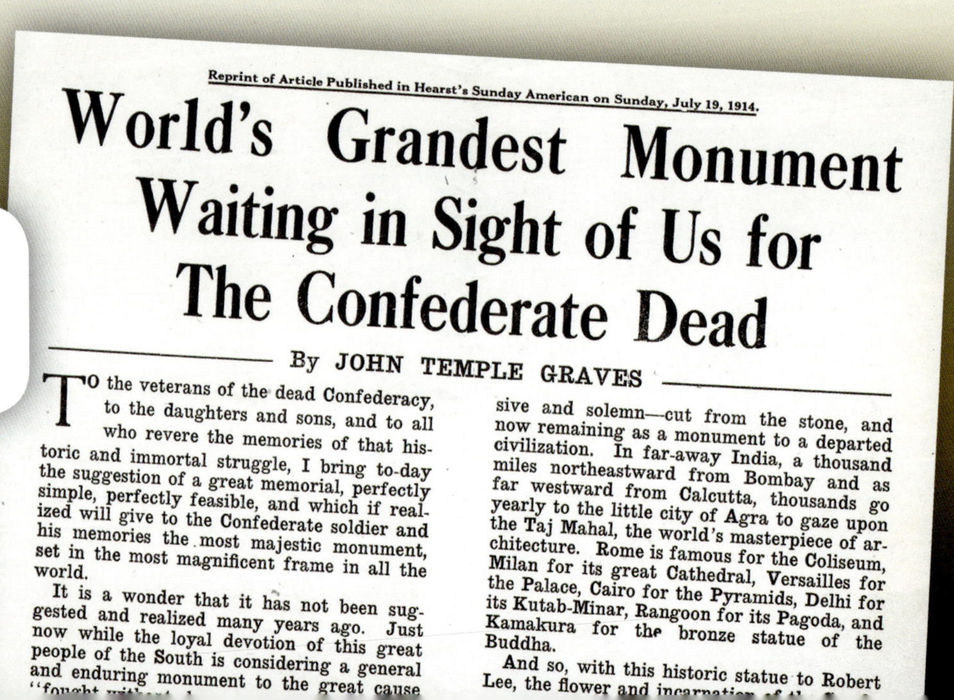

Reprint of Article Published in Hearst's Sunday American on Sunday, July 19, 1914.

World's Grandest Monument Waiting in Sight of Us for The Confederate Dead

By JOHN TEMPLE GRAVES

TO the veterans of the dead Confederacy, to the daughters and sons, and to all who revere the memories of that historic and immortal struggle, I bring to-day the suggestion of a great memorial, perfectly simple, perfectly feasible, and which if realized will give to the Confederate soldier and his memories the most majestic monument, set in the most magnificent frame in all the world.

It is a wonder that it has not been suggested and realized many years ago. Just now while the loyal devotion of this great people of the South is considering a general and enduring monument to the great cause "fought without ...

sive and solemn—cut from the stone, and now remaining as a monument to a departed civilization. In far-away India, a thousand miles northeastward from Bombay and as far westward from Calcutta, thousands go yearly to the little city of Agra to gaze upon the Taj Mahal, the world's masterpiece of architecture. Rome is famous for the Coliseum, Milan for its great Cathedral, Versailles for the Palace, Cairo for the Pyramids, Delhi for its Kutab-Minar, Rangoon for its Pagoda, and Kamakura for the bronze statue of the Buddha.

And so, with this historic statue to Robert Lee, the flower and incarnation ...

OTHER PERSPECTIVES

Speechmakers are not the only ones with a point of view. The people who create secondary sources have their own perspectives, too. This can lead to multiple ways of looking at the same speech. Studying a variety of primary and secondary sources gives a wider view of an issue. These materials could be from the same time period or in response to the speech.

IN FAVOR OF LYNCHING

John Temple Graves was a newspaper journalist from Atlanta, Georgia. He believed that laws were not enough to stop crimes against women. It was his point of view that lynching was a more effective way to protect them. He was invited to speak in Chautauqua, New York, on August 11, 1903. The audience was mainly Americans from northern states. Graves tried to convince them that lynching was the only way to keep African American men from attacking white women. He chose his words carefully to play on the audience's emotions. He claimed that lynching actually prevented crimes. Graves argued that it kept people from becoming so angry with African Americans that they wiped out the whole race.

Speaker: *John Temple Graves*
Audience: *Mainly Americans from northern states*
Date: *August 11, 1903*

"*The **mob** stands today as the most potential **bulwark** between the women of the South and such a **carnival of crime** as would **infuriate** the world and **precipitate the annihilation** of the Negro race.*"

- **Unlike Wells, Graves did not see this as a negative term**
- **Wall of protection**
- **Word choice suggests that African Americans took pleasure in breaking laws**
- **Fill with rage**
- **Bring about the destruction**

Three boys protest the integration of Black and white students in taxpayer supported schools in Tennessee in 1956.

An anti-integration rally in Little Rock, Arkansas, in 1959. These rallies attracted mobs of white protestors, much like lynchings did a half century earlier.

DIGGING DEEPER

How do people's different backgrounds influence their perspectives?

ANOTHER VIEW OF LYNCHING

Frederick Douglass was a civil rights activist like Ida B. Wells. His experiences were different from hers. Douglass had escaped slavery and was in his forties by the start of the American Civil War. This shaped his own perspective. Douglass shared Wells's view that lynching was a crime that needed to be stopped. However, in a speech called "The Lessons of the Hour," he argued that as a threat to order, lynching was a risk to all Americans. He gave this famous address on Tuesday, January 9, 1894. The Metropolitan African Methodist Episcopal Church in Washington, D.C., hosted him as a speaker. The audience was mainly African American members of the church and their guests.

Frederick Douglass claimed formerly enslaved people were not at fault for any problems the United States faced with them.

Speaker: *Frederick Douglass*
Audience: *Metropolitan African Methodist Episcopal Church members and their guests*
Date: *January 9, 1894*

> *"...the* ***sport of mob violence and murder*** *is not only a disgrace and scandal to that* ***particular section*** *but a* ***menace*** *to the peace and security of the people of the whole country... increasing not only in the number of its victims, but in its* ***frantic rage and savage extravagance***. ***Lawless vengeance*** *is beginning to be visited upon white men as well as black... The* ***contagion is spreading****...if permitted to go on it threatens to destroy all respect for law and order not only in the South, but in all parts of our country..."*

- Douglass shared Wells's view on what lynching was
- The South
- Threat
- Referred to the extreme violence
- Revenge outside the legal system
- Compared lynching to an infection

READ IT

Read the full text of Douglass's speech: **https://bit.ly/3dJVCiN**

CHAPTER 4

INFLUENCES THEN AND NOW

Ida B. Wells made it difficult for Americans to deny that lynching was a crime. In 1909, there were about 80 lynchings in the United States. More have likely gone unreported. The official number lowered each year after that. By the mid-1930s, there were fewer than 10 lynchings per year. The mobs became smaller, more secretive groups. They still claimed to seek justice. In 1981, Ku Klux Klan members lynched Michael Donald. The African American teenager was picked randomly after another man was found innocent of killing a police officer. This crime proved Wells's old argument that lynching was murder used to terrorize. It was still being used to intimidate African Americans.

The Ku Klux Klan members who lynched Michael Donald in 1981 were found guilty of murder.

Michael Donald's mother Beulah Mae Donald attends a news conference after winning a case against the Ku Klux Klan.

DIGGING DEEPER

If the audience is not swayed by an argument, do you think that means the speech was a failure? Why or why not?

FIGHTING UNTIL THE END

Ida B. Wells carried on her work as a civil rights activist for two more decades after giving her "Lynching, Our National Crime" speech. She worked for the National Equal Rights League to fight for women in the workplace. Wells lived to see American women get the right to vote in 1920. However, she did not convince the U.S. government to make lynching a country-wide crime. She died from kidney disease on March 25, 1931. She was 68 years old.

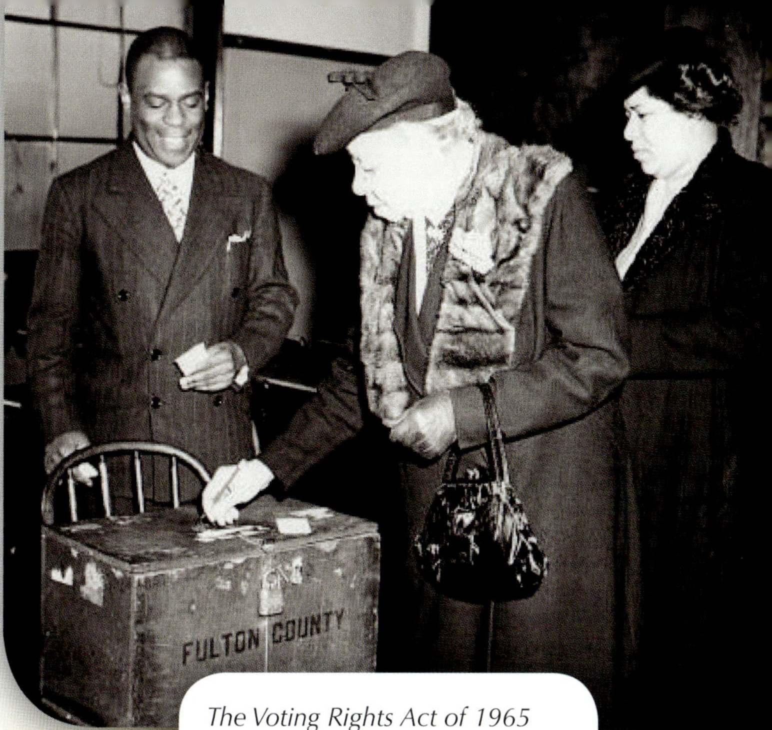

The Voting Rights Act of 1965 allowed African Americans to exercise their right to vote by removing legal barriers set in place by state and local governments.

LYNCHING BECOMES A CRIME

More than 5,000 people have been lynched in the United States. It is unknown how many cases went unreported. About three-quarters of the victims were Black. Over the years, the U.S. Congress rejected almost 200 **bills** to end lynching. It finally became a federal crime on December 19, 2018. Lynching is now considered a **hate crime**. That same year, the National Memorial for Peace and Justice opened in Montgomery, Alabama. Over 800 coffin-sized and -shaped monuments hang from its ceiling. They stand for the counties and states in which lynchings took place. In 2000, James Allen collected historical images of lynchings. He published them in a book called *Without Sanctuary*. Seeing these primary sources shocked modern audiences. This showed how much perspectives changed from the previous century.

Ida B. Wells's name is now found on many schools across the United States, such as this high school in San Francisco.

MODERN PERSPECTIVE

Politicians must be able to make persuasive speeches. On Friday, September 7, 2018, former U.S. president Barack Obama spoke to the students at the University of Illinois at Urbana-Champaign. The media covered the event, so he also had a national audience. The purpose of Obama's speech was to convince young Americans to vote. He wanted them to support the Democrats in the November elections. His perspective was that the current government, led by President Donald Trump, was pulling the country backward. One theme of Obama's speech was fighting against dividing citizens based on their differences.

> "*...there's been at least rough agreement among the overwhelming majority of Americans that our country is strongest when everybody's treated fairly...And even though* ***your generation is the most diverse in history, with a greater acceptance and celebration of our differences than ever before, those are the kinds of conditions*** *that are* ***ripe for exploitation*** *by politicians who have* ***no compunction and no shame*** *about tapping into America's dark history of racial and ethnic and religious division...This is a big country...People have different points of view...The idea that, well, you know there's racism in America so I'm not going to bother voting...* ***Better's always worth fighting for****...With each new step we take in the direction of fairness and justice and equality and opportunity, hope spreads.*"

Speaker: *Barack Obama*
Audience: *Students at the University of Illinois at Urbana-Champaign*
Date: *September 7, 2018*

Students in the audience were used to interacting with people from many backgrounds

Economic and international threats that create insecurity

Easy to misuse and take advantage of

No guilt or regrets

Obama contrasted pitting people against one another with working together

WATCH IT

See President Obama speaking at the University of Illinois: **www.youtube.com/watch?v=AFWEJssr29k**

In 2007, Barack Obama kicked off his presidential campaign in Springfield, Illinois. He chose it because of its ties to President Abraham Lincoln.

DIGGING DEEPER

Current technologies can help spread ideas widely. Do you think videos of speeches are as effective as live speeches? Why or why not?

A LEADER WORTH REMEMBERING

Ida B. Wells was a trailblazer. She was a female activist at a time when women were not viewed as equal to men. Her family thrived after being freed from slavery. She became the first woman co-owner of a newspaper in a major city. These were all significant successes. Through her speech, she showed that people do not need to accept the way things are. Before Wells began investigating and writing about lynching, many people believed the victims deserved it. Wells fought to show her country the true motives behind these murders—even as her activism risked her own life.

The National Memorial for Peace and Justice is located in Montgomery, Alabama. The memorial features 800 steel monuments to mark each county in the U.S. where a lynching took place. An inner reflection space was built to honor Ida B. Wells. The memorial and its museum are dedicated to the legacy of enslaved Black people and those terrorized and hurt by racial segregation and brutality. Staff continue Ida's work by researching contemporary racial terror, placing monuments in communities where lynchings took place, and challenging current racial injustices.

BIBLIOGRAPHY

INTRODUCTION

"Biographies: Ida B. Wells." PBS. www.pbs.org/blackpress/news_bios/wells.html

Corley, Cheryl. "Springfield, Ill., Marks Centenary Of Riots." National Public Radio. www.npr.org/templates/story/story.php?storyId=93606402.

"Emancipation Proclamation." History.com. www.history.com/topics/american-civil-war/emancipation-proclamation

Gannon, Megan. "In Land of Lincoln, Long-Buried Traces of a Race Riot Come to the Surface." *Smithsonian Magazine*, January 7, 2019. https://bit.ly/2A3EaaV

Hannah-Jones, Nikole. "When Ida B. Wells Married, It Was a Page One Story." *The New York Times*, January 23, 2017. https://nyti.ms/2ZcbHbB

"Ida B. Wells Biography." Biography. www.biography.com/activist/ida-b-wells

National Negro Conference. *Proceedings of the National Negro Conference*. 1909.

Rudwick, Elliott M. "The National Negro Committee Conference of 1909." *The Phylon Quarterly*, 1957.

Wells, Ida B. "Lynching Our National Crime – June 1, 1909." Iowa State University. https://bit.ly/3fSPjKQ

CHAPTER 1

"Biography Examines Life of Ida B. Wells." National Public Radio. www.npr.org/templates/story/story.php?storyId=89109212

Fahnestock, Jeanne. *Rhetorical Style: The Uses of Language in Persuasion*. New York: Oxford University, 2011.

Frazer-Carroll. "Hair discrimination is intertwined with racism. Let's follow California, and ban it." *The Guardian*, July 8, 2019. https://bit.ly/382NyIh

"Ida B. Wells: A Passion for Justice." California Newsreel. newsreel.org/video/ida-b-wells

"NAACP." History.com. www.history.com/topics/civil-rights-movement/naacp

"Our History." Henry Street Settlement. www.henrystreet.org/about/our-history

Peavey, Linda and Ursula Smith. "Ida B. Wells' Determined Quest for Equality." *Memphis*, April 9, 2019. https://bit.ly/31fEwGB

"Primary Sources." University of California Irving Libraries. www.lib.uci.edu/introduction-primary-sources

"Primary Sources: What Are They?" Teaching History. https://bit.ly/2BCj0kD

"Primary vs. Secondary Sources." BMCC Library. lib1.bmcc.cuny.edu/help/sources

"Using Primary Sources." United States Library of Congress. www.loc.gov/teachers/usingprimarysources

Weida, Stacy and Karl Stolley. "Using Rhetorical Strategies for Persuasion." Purdue Online Writing Lab. owl.english.purdue.edu/owl/resource/588/04

CHAPTER 2

"Ku Klux Klan." *Encyclopaedia Britannica*. www.britannica.com/topic/Ku-Klux-Klan

Logan, Shirley Wilson. "Ida B. Wells, 'Lynch Law in All Its Phases' (13 February 1893)." *Voices of Democracy*, 2007. voicesofdemocracy.umd.edu/wp-content/uploads/2010/07/logan-wells.pdf

"Natural Rights." Constitutional Rights Foundation. www.crf-usa.org/foundations-of-our-constitution/natural-rights.html

Wells, Ida B. "Lynch Law in America—January 1900." Archives of Women's Political Communication, Iowa State University. awpc.cattcenter.iastate.edu/2017/03/21/lynch-law-in-america-january-1900

Wells, Ida B. *Southern Horrors: Lynch Law in All Its Phases*. New York: The New York Age Print, 1892.

CHAPTER 3

Abbott, Dorothy, ed. *Mississippi Writers: Reflections of Childhood and Youth*. Oxford: University Press of Mississippi, 1986.

"Alfreda Wells discusses her mother, Ida B. Wells-Barnett, and her book 'Crusade for Justice'." Studs Terkel Radio Archive https://bit.ly/31fBX7u

DeCosta-Willis, Miriam. "Ida B. Wells-Barnett." Tennessee Encyclopedia. https://tennesseeencyclopedia.net/entries/ida-b-wells-barnett

Douglass, Frederick. "The Lessons of the Hour" Speech by Frederick Douglass, January 9, 1894. State Historical Society of Iowa. https://bit.ly/31ichHd

"He Defends Lynch Law." *The New York Times*, August 12, 1903. timesmachine.nytimes.com/timesmachine/1903/08/12/102017453.pdf

Williamson, Joel. *The Crucible of Race: Black/White Relations in the American South Since Emancipation*. New York: Oxford University Press, 1984.

CHAPTER 4

Blakemore, Erin. "The 1981 Lynching that Bankrupted an Alabama KKK." History.com. www.history.com/news/kkk-lynching-mother-justice

"History of Lynchings." NAACP. www.naacp.org/history-of-lynchings

Masur, Louis P. "Why It Took a Century to Pass an Anti-Lynching Law." *The Washington Post*, December 28, 2018.

"President Barack Obama speaks at the University of Illinois, September 7, 2018." YouTube.com. www.youtube.com/watch?v=AFWEJssr29k

"Read transcript of former President Obama's speech, blasting President Trump." USA Today. https://bit.ly/382A1AQ

"The Legacy of Ida B. Wells." The University of Chicago Library. https://bit.ly/3g2urRH

LEARNING MORE

BOOKS

Hinman, Bonnie. *Eternal Vigilance: The Story of Ida B. Wells-Barnett.* Greensboro: Morgan Reynolds Publishing, 2010.

Santella, Andrew. *The NAACP: An Organization Working to End Discrimination.* North Mankato: The Child's World, 2003

Uhl, Xina M. and Tonya Buell. *A Primary Source Investigation of Slavery.* New York: Rosen Central, 2019.

Wishinsky, Frieda. *Freedom Heroines # 4.* New York: Scholastic, 2012.

WEBSITES

Dig deeper into primary and secondary resources: **https://sccollege.edu/Library/Pages/primarysources.aspx**

Read about Ida B. Wells's life: **www.nps.gov/people/idabwells.htm**

Find out more about the issues on the Equal Justice Initiative website: **https://eji.org**

GLOSSARY

activist A person who works to bring about social or political change
address A speech written or directed to a specific group of people
analogy A similarity between two things from which a comparison is made
analyze To examine critically to understand causes and meaning
argument A discussion or debate involving different points of view
bills Proposed laws
biographer Someone who writes an account of someone elses' life
civil rights The rights of citizens to political and social freedoms and equality
Civil War A war (1861–65) between the northern U.S. states, known as the Union, and the Confederate states of the South, in which the Union won
condemn To express complete disapproval of something or someone
Confederate Army The army of the 11 southern states that seceded from the U.S. in 1860–61, and fought against the Union during the Civil War
credibility To be trusted and believable
discriminatory Something that is unfair
disenfranchisement To deprive or take away a person's right to vote
Emancipation Proclamation A presidential proclamation that freed enslaved African Americans in Confederate states during the Civil War
hate crime A crime motivated by racial or other prejudice
hyperbole Obvious exaggeration
hypocrite Someone who claims to have moral or ethical standards or beliefs but who does not conform to these beliefs in their behavior
indignities Treatment that denies a person honor or respect and causes them to feel pain
inequality The state of being unequal in rights, status, or opportunities
intended Designed or meant for a particular reason or purpose
investigative reporter A journalist or someone who carries out thorough research to discover and examine facts and then write about them
metaphor A figure of speech where a phrase is used to stand for something else
militia A military force made up of civilians
mob An unruly crowd
notable Worthy of attention or notice
personification Giving human qualities to an animal, object, or idea
persuasion Convincing or urging someone to do something by appealing to reason
persuasive Intended to persuade
prejudice A preconcieved opinion not based on reason or fact
racial discrimination Making judgments based on the color of a person's skin, rather than on merit
rape A crime of having sexual intercourse with someone against their will
segregated Set apart along racial lines
simile A figure of speech in which two things that are not alike are compared
systemic Widespread and often planned
tone A particular attitude or feeling
U.S. Library of Congress The research library of the United States Congress that also serves as a national library
white supremacist Someone who believes white people are superior to people of color
yellow fever A disease spread by mosquitoes

INDEX

ABOUT THE AUTHOR

Rebecca Sjonger is the author of over 50 non-fiction books for young people. American history is one of her favorite subjects to write about. She loves the challenge of separating facts from fiction while researching.